On the Make Again/
Otra Vez en la Movida

New and Collected Poems by Jim Sagel

For Carol—
Best wishes
from Jim Sagel
4/11/95

On the Make Again/ Otra Vez en la Movida

New and Collected Poems by Jim Sagel

West End Press

"Foreplay and French Fries" was originally published by Mango Publications (Chicano Chapbook Series), San Jose, California, 1981.

"Hablando de Brujas (y la gente de antes)" was originally published by Place of Herons Press, Austin, Texas, 1981.

"Little Eyes" (from the book *Small Bones/Little Eyes*) was originally published by Duck Down Press, Fallon, Nevada, 1981.

"Los Cumpleaños de doña Agueda" was originally published by Place of Herons Press, Austin, Texas, 1984.

Poems from HAROLD M. ES RATA originally appeared in the following magazines and journals: SUNTRACKS, GREENFIELD REVIEW, PUERTO DEL SOL, NEW MEXICO HUMANITIES REVIEW, MANGO, PEMBROKE, CONCEPTIONS SOUTHWEST, CONTENTS UNDER PRESSURE, SECOND CHICANO COLLECTION, EL TECOLOTE, REVISTA RIO BRAVO, CEREMONY OF BROTHERHOOD (ACADEMIA), BRUSHFIRE, ROCKY MOUNTAIN REVIEW, ORO MADRE, PENOLA, DACOTAH TERRITORY, NEW KAURI, RESIEMBRA, PHANTASM, and VIA IMAGINACIÓN.

ISBN 0-931122-54-6

Cover art: *El Bastonero* by Frederico M. Vigil. This painting was part of the national U.S. touring exhibit "Expresiones Hispanicos" in 1989.
Photograph of Jim Sagel by Theresa Archuleta-Sagel.
Design by Michael Reed.
Typography by Prototype.

Our thanks to Tony and Enrique for their help.

WEST END PRESS
P.O. Box 27334
Albuquerque, NM 87125

TABLE OF CONTENTS

Para mis maestros
y todos mis estudiantes

FOREPLAY AND FRENCH FRIES

REINA DE REINAS

Reina de reinas
she was Miss Crusader
  favorite "All-around Girl"
  of the Holy Cross Fighting Conquistadores
and School Sweetheart
and head cheerleader
and first runner-up for Prom Queen
  (the theme that year, you know, was "Moonlight and
  Roses" and they had a plywood wishing well decorated
  with red and white streamers and red construction
  paper bells it took the art classes two months to
  prepare and hundreds of red balloons and the most
  beautiful tissue roses)
but she has "puta" inked in by her picture
in the high school annual
  the same book she edited
and appeared in as "Most Attractive Girl"
and who easily had the longest index list
  of picture credits in the back
where nearly the entire school population had written:
  "To a real cool chick" and "God bless you"
but what I wonder is why all those wishful quarters
down the tin-foiled well never worked
  and why it's always the "Most Likely to Succeed"
who end up with six kids
  an abusive husband
and "puta" by their names in the yearbook

HOMECOMING

Not much has changed in twenty years
at Sacred Heart School
The identical Lysol stench seeps through the halls
"Fuck" and "cabrón" are still big on the restroom walls
and Clarence remains a "joto" after all these years
Decades of plaster and paint
now hide the hole we drilled through the wall
with our dull navajitas
pretending to see Mary Lou "abajar los panties"
in the girls' restroom
because she was the only sixth grader with breasts
Then we'd repeat the stale dirty jokes
and laugh at "Peter-fuck-her-faster" and "Mary-lay-still"
in our sole sanctuary
from the twisted wrath of the monjas
The jokes are the same no doubt
though progress has even trickled
into this chalk-dusted seventh circle
of God's educational hell
And now the guys—Michael tells me—gather beside the latrines
to play a pirated cassette recording
of Cheech and Chong's "Up in Smoke"
and the girls—who once traded a knee-numbing kick
for an adolescent hug-and-tackle—
now coolly charge two bits a kiss
and cash in their bodies
at Duran's candy store across the street
Yes—Duran's is still there
but somehow it no longer resembles heaven—
real heaven, not the perverse nunnish version
that would have you praying on wooden knees for eternity
unless, of course, you wished to plunge
where flames licked tender bodies
and charred delicate bones
We knew the horrible details
in all their gruesome intricacy
and hell still haunts the place
You can feel it lurking around every corner
behind each blackboard and map of the Holy Land
but I still hear the crisp, screeching laughter

that shook hell into playground dust
and I return to my car reassured
Nothing has changed
The black wings beat harmlessly against the swinging
    sun
and the only thing that bothers me really
is that the giant slide somehow shrank

FOREPLAY AND FRENCH FRIES

A mufflerless caravan of pregnant pink Chevies
jacked-up GMC tanks
and menacing smoke-glassed black Trans-Ams
leaks down Riverside Drive
lights blinking in the buzzed twilight

Westside homeboys spit insults
at scowling lowrider Chimayosos—
Terminal loners weave across lanes
with Armageddon in their eyes

High school queens giggle in VWs
silly on big brother's mota
in the back row of the Tastee-Freeze parking lot
while Tiny Morrie wails:
"Me llaman el asesino por ahi"
from a chorus of radios
and motors mumble a macho counterpoint
at the Happy Days Liquor drive-up window
where fake-IDed adolescents queue up
for a quart of Southern Comfort

The air is thick and ripe and sweet
like first sex on imitation zebra-pelt seats
and everyone's waiting for something to happen—
the sudden spray of shattered glass
the explosion between the thighs
the vision of the Virgin Mother dancing
just beyond the furred dice
that dangle from the rear-view mirror

But it's all foreplay and french fries
and the cruise will never end—
Anticipation gnaws away at the night
leaving nothing but bare bones

BLONDIE

she cruises down Fairview Lane in
  her white Pinto tripping on
    the jams with a stoned load
    of locos mellowed to the max
            slender
            and gazelle-legged
            she runs through green aspens
            just ahead of the wind
and she laughs when they crank
  up the cassette and say I didn't
  know you were Indian do you know
    how to talk the language
            she sings
            grandmother melodies
            to the crescent-horned moon
            impaled on the lonely black mesa
and they circulate three simultaneous
  joints and ask how come you never
  hang around the pueblo and make
    pottery like your mother to sell
            her hands
            become birds
            feathering blue nugget rain
            from the crystal Puyé sky
and she nods time to the swell of
  sound that billows in unison with
  the sweet smoke fogging her mirrored
  sunglasses in the Safeway parking lot
            angry drums
            echo four hundred silent
            years deep and her black eyes
            flash open all at once
    remembering everything

SU FAMILIA ES BUENA GENTE

but you've got to remember
when he killed that state chota
it was not out of premeditated malice—
just a casual shooting
that's all it was
like finishing off the coyote snarled in a trap
routine—
like the rattler bites and bubonic plague
that regularly usher souls off these high red mesas—
sudden—
like the drunken pickup shattering
into cattleguard reinforcement posts—
like liver-piercing pocketknives
at wedding dance fights—
and though he already had a reputation
for throwing chingazos at a moment's notice
su familia es buena gente
and everyone feels sorry for his mother
"tan buena mujer que es"
the vecinos sigh
as wary tíos sign over their ranchitos
on property bonds for a man they'd rather see
rot in the pinta
"cómo ha sufrido esa pobre"
the parishioners whisper
as she hobbles up to the altar
for her weekly unleavened wafer
that's somehow supposed to resurrect dead sons

HABLANDO DE BRUJAS
(y la gente de antes)

PARA DON JUAN BORREGO

y ya se fue el señor Borrego
with his gentle sheepherder's memory
that stretched back a los días mágicos de antes

if it would make any difference
I'd say he simply went riding over the still llano
on the broken old yegua y desapareció
tal vez queriendo recoger un borreguito
abandonado

pero ya comió la familia
y se fue
se fue como siempre
and already his memory evaporates into the grey skies
over Los Angeles and Dallas

CORTANDO ALFALFA

just enough rain
to force me off the tractor and under the oaks
with the five-year-old boy
who'd been trailing the rastrillo all morning

I tell him
the hay will pick up too much dirt
if I continue to rake now
and the bales will come out polvorosos
like those a couple of years back
that made the horse sick

we chew on lemitas
and pitch a few aimless rocks
at the bucket on the fence
while he tells me about fistfights outside the church
and the logging truck that hit the turn too fast
spilling its cuartones on a volkswagen bus
full of hippies

"¿De veras?" I find myself repeating
"Pues, sí mano" my compañero replies every time

when we see the rain's not likely to lift
we decide to head back on foot for the house
on the way we pull up some ragweed for the pig
and get our pants wet to the knee
cutting across the field of a man
who took his cancer-ridden wife out of the hospital
and allowed her to slowly scream to death
because the pain pills
were too damned expensive

HABLANDO DE BRUJAS

a bare bulb
battled off the August darkness
as we sat beside pilas de chile y calabazas
hablando de brujas
    y la gente de antes
terrified and fascinated a la vez

the sweet low talk rolled on
como las acequias coloradas del Río Chama
and I felt myself sinking back
    no longer resisting
y mi alma se fue desenredando casi a la luna

EL OSITO

Gritos de oso
    sizzle through the pines and encinos
as you swirl the rifle
at the widening black eyes
se cae como un troncón de cedro
    shredding the morning moon
while your daughter whimpers
at the edge of a rippling silence

Uno de los ositos se queda huérfano
wrapped in terror on a towering branch
pero el otro que se trampó abajo de la mamá
rides back with you to the cabin
where in time you have him on your leg
    like an aboriginal ventriloquist
y nadien pero nadien se arrima a molestar

Until one April morning your wife
en una pasada de la escoba
    receives a playful bat and four purple scars
and the osito is off to the zoo
"Ya no puede estar vivo"
    you tell me
miles of Aprils away
searching your huge animal hands

YA MERO

"Mañanaba uno en lo escuro—¡sonamagón, qué friazo!—
y en el carro de caballo no había heater ni nada de eso"

"Seguro que no"

"Me mandaba enpapá con su orden a Española—solo
y muy chiquito todavía—pos, ni quitaba yo los
frenos porque no los podía poner. Me tardaba tres
días pa' llegar—y dormía en el bosque. Hoy en día
no podía uno mandar a un muchacho solo tan lejos"

"Ni a la plaza por cigarritos"

"Sí—ya todo va pa' quince. Los vecinos no ayudan
unos a los otros como antes"

"Solamente por pago"

And we roll back through "los días de las goteras"
when rain fell tan seguido que pasaba por los techos
    the time el difunto Frutoso hitched
un tiro de caballos on the old Ford para prenderlo
and the years cuando no había dinero pero los centavos sí
    valían

You've heard it all a hundred times
yet you sit entranced as the words fade in the distance
    over the twisted Camels and empty coffee cups
hasta que ya mero—ya mero llegas

cuando los nietos entran con un golpe
shrieking like televisions
    taking over
hablando puro inglés

15

THOSE ARE COYOTE'S EYES ALL RIGHT

Uncle Steven weaves the red-and-white river reeds
into ever-widening suns
        while Grasshopper Legs
pierces purple kernels
silently stringing a double corn necklace

There's a violent fire of ocote and green cedar
in the deep mud fireplace
a windy night outside
        moonless
yet this boy still fools
with the broken receiver on the ancient TV
cursing the sizzling snowy screen
while Uncle sings an old song
        that no one listens to

Finally with eyes desperate as Coyote's
when he's spotted a rotted chicken
set in the steel jaws
        of a Sears gopher trap
he bursts out into the black November night
where brujas twist and flutter
like chispas out of the chimneys

Later at the Chamita bar
over a dozen Schlitz and whiskeys
he tells me how he served a tour in Vietnam
        with the Marines in 66
got shot up twice and volunteered again
how he'd personally killed
        "hundreds of fuckin' gooks"
how he still has nightmares after so many years
is on a steady diet of librium
and probably always will be

And I'm thinking about Uncle Steven
tying up a basket for some Texas tourist
        in the faltering light
and the dark polished necklace
ending up at the bottom
of a granddaughter's drawer

Yeah, those are Coyote's eyes all right
buried in the revolving Hamm's light
    on the cantina wall
but they're not the laughing eyes
that told impossible tales around the table
about the time he stole three sheep
and fucked the shepherd's daughter
    for good measure

No, those eyes look more like the time
he forgot to watch
and got smashed by a truck

LA VECINA

nos platicaba de la llorona
and halfway through the cuento
with her eyes rolled back
    white as death
and her chicken hawk voice peeled and piercing
    temblábamos
thoroughly convinced
she was the celebrated hag of the Chamita bridge
herself

siempre había bizcochitos o empanaditas
    pan fresco o tortillas mexicanas
en su cocinita llena de luz
and she'd serve us her homemade cherry wine
pero nomás llegaba el jefe
y ella quitaba las copas devolada
    unceremoniously chugging down
lo que quedaba del vino

nunca aceptó las estampas
survived instead on the hard roots and twisted elotes
she coaxed out of her stubborn huertita
    siempre mandándonos la mitad
de su pepinos y calabazas

y cuando se interesó en los ceramics
at the Senior Citizens
y no había nadien para llevarla
    aprendió a arrear
taught herself to drive at sixty-eight years of age
    y sacó licencia
nomás que al principio she'd forget
the order of the gears
así que los puso nombres para acordar:
    Cochina, Cagada, Cabrona—
    First, Second and Third
(she always remembered reverse)

pero como uno pone y Dios al fin dispone
llegó el hielo
      y el malvado invierno se la llevó
leaving only a fading scent of anís y cerezas
in the dark kitchen

esta noche le rezan el velorio
but I'm not going to pray—
never was nothing
that could hold that woman down

¡Andale—Cochina, Cagada, Cabrona—
Vamos pa'l cielo!

ESTO SE DICE A LAS MUCHITAS QUE SE LASTIMAN

sana sana
        (when it comes to mending
                broken eyes
colita de rana
        the only remedio outside of
                growing flowers
si no sanas hoy
                is a broken strand of your
                        grandmother's words
sanarás mañana
        that tumble musically
                out of your chest)

¿ME QUIERES?

Allá en el río
    escondida de su papá
ella se junta con él
a llenar su bote para la cena
y platicar entre los encinos

flor de orégano
    corta él para ella
y pasa un rato
pescando truchas
con la mano

pero pronto el sol
    se va bajando
y ella tiene que irse

"¿Me quieres?" pregunta él

"Sí, mucho" responde ella

LLAMAME EL PADRE

"Llámame el padre, esposo—
ya me muero"
    she cried, clinging to the bedpost

"Pero ¿qué tienes, mujer?
¿Qué te pasa?"
    preguntó el hombre
bien asustado
    squinting in the blinding 2 a.m.
    electric daylight

"Yo no sé.
Es la cosa que siempre me da,
pero esta noche no se quita"
    y se levantó de repente
for the bed was about to spin her off
into the void

"Te llevo al hospital—¡Vamos!"

"Ya no.
Llámame el padre—
y paga los cinco pesos que debo a mi hermanita."

She inched into the kitchen for water
grim as a martyr
ignoring her husband
    (ya apenado de verdad)
gritando—"¡Vamos al hospital!"

cuando
vido ella el vaso
y se acordó del vino que su hija
    le había regalado (for her eternal insomnia)
y se acordó cómo había bebido
todo el vaso

"Acuéstate y no me hagas aprecio . . ."
    she waved him away—
"¡No tengo más que la borrachera!"

SCARS

three batos from Brewtown barrio
pass around a permanent roach
their tattooed teeshirted arms
glistening in the sun
while a couple of San Felipe boys
thumb the impossible ride downtown

a greyed-out wino mumbles to the lines in his palms
and an aging hippie buries his bearded head
in his hands slumped up against the white brick wall
of the Blood Plasma Donor Center

scars cut deep around here
like trail bikes slicing up
the adolescent face of Santa Clara Peak
or the heartbound 67 promnight initials
etched into Puyé sandstone
millimeters from ancient petroglyphs

like cloistered condominiums drilled into the bedrock
of the Sangre de Cristos
the scars of needles track down the dark delicate arms
of those who sell their blood
to survive

EL OJO

Dicen que tenía el mal ojo

Izque nació asina
with one black eye wandering free of the other
locked into an unfocused gaze

When he walked into a room
se enfermaban los niños
y soltaban llorando las muchachitas
 they say if a man dared to return that frozen stare
alguna cosa le iba a pasar de seguro
perhaps his horse would go lame or his pig might die
dicen que su hermano perdió su mujer
 a causa de ese ojo

Al fin se quedó solito
out of sight with a bottle in a one-room cabin
allí lo hallaron muerto
y allí lo dejaron
 in the rocky soil of the Sangre de Cristos

Pero los viejos dicen
que tenía el ojo todavía abierto en la muerte
and that they buried him boca abajo
 just to be certain

CO-OP

these women stringing corn necklaces
and gossiping in Tewa
don't spin around on the earth's axis
    like you and I
they are fixed solid in a still place
where only their delicate sinewy hands move

Mrs. Jones walks in from four hundred years ago
floating on a silver-and-black cane
she's brought meaty red chile and bread
    only the names have changed
and the building

glazed brick has replaced packed blood-browned mud
and an occasional tourist interrupts
asking in a cacophonous twang
    for the bathroom
or the price of a pot

but the place is the same
    ancient as the Euphrates
the corn beads are blue and yellow drops
of dissolving time
and the voices echo
    bouncing back centuries
even if they're only talking about who's pregnant
    and who's divorced

suddenly Uncle Steven appears around the corner
with a trilingual anecdote about his horse
    and Okie son-in-law
and the women burst into laughter
that bellows to the ceiling
like a boiling explosion of sparrows

WILLY

"You can always tell a woman who's had a kid"
    Willy says—
"Her ass drops just like a sack of flour"
and he should know
having eyed asses since he was big enough
to kick his leg up over a pony's back

"Hey Jim"
    he yells across the room—
"come look at my knives"
and he shows me an outrageous collection
of daggers, penknives, switchblades and
    hog-butcherers—
this gentle man who couldn't even put
the pet cat out of her misery
after those drunks hit her
and he proceeds to shave the hair on his arm
showing off the razor edge
he spends endless hours accomplishing

and then it's the gun collection
and we fondle his magnum pistol
twelve-gauge shotgun, British 303
and mafioso breakdown-22
while he tells me how last Saturday
he was out riding his mare when he came upon a car
under that old álamo down by the arroyo
"and there were some high school kids
screwin' right there—and she was on top of him
and boy they were really goin' to it"
and we laugh as he catapults his grandson
playfully in his thick arms
and fragilely placing him on the linoleum floor
hands the two-year-old a plastic bat

and after painstakingly demonstrating the correct stance
pitches him a tennis ball
for a little spontaneous batting practice
in the living room
and Willy, who was quite a catcher in his day
reveals his most carefully guarded
little league coaching secret to me
"You know I tell those little guys
not to squeeze that bat so hard—
just grab ahold of it
like they hold their dick
when they're going to take a piss—
and you know they really like that"

and he shows me his leather hat
one of his several thousand favorite possessions
the one with the silver and coral pin
he made for the Indian Market
Willy's always got something in his hands
always handling something
whether it's a horse's reins, a weaving shuttle
a 2 × 4 or an obnoxious drunk
I imagine he even laughs in his sleep

"Hey Jim—let's go to the horse races
over in Alcalde next week"
        and he tells me
about how the guys from the pueblo
and all around the valley get together to run their horses
and drink beer
and how those guys from Alcalde sure do cheat a lot
but one time he made 150 bucks on his palomino
and you should have seen how big his cousin's eyes got
"It's only fifty cents"
        he says as I'm stepping out the door
"and you get to see all the races
and a fistfight too"

JUANITO

"The body of Christ"
   declared the padre

"Hello"
   Juanito replied
politely making God's acquaintance
and the sixth grade gang in the back of the church
gleefully punched each other's knees
for, you see, Juanito had not yet made
his first holy communion
but had joined the pious procession down the aisle
at the older boys' bidding

It was the scandal of the year
at Sacred Heart School
and everybody talked about it on the swings
and laughed about it down the slide

The monjas gave an ominous lecture
on the sacredness of the host
and the boys were punished
with a few rosario-crammed recesses
when one of the conspirators broke
under the threat of eternal hellfire

And Juanito?
Well, it changed his life forever—
he became an insurance salesman
ran for the school board
bought a boat and a camper
and was never polite to God again

HIGH SCHOOL HEAVEN

It was the perfect wedding
a marriage ordained in high school heaven
Carmela—Holy Cross Head Cheerleader
and Fidel—Captain of the Basketball Team
After the wedding they moved in with his mom
y el Fidel pescó un jale
with the old man while Carmela stayed home
cuidando los muchachos
y qué curioso que después de tantos años—
con la familia grande ya
already in high school themselves—
Fidel still feels cheated by that final buzzer
that froze his best shot in midair
and Carmela daydreams of drawing erotic cheers
from a frenzied crowd
sitting in the Penny Pincher Laundromat
on a hot stale sábado in limp rollers
watching the máquina spin
and trading her quarters for a little more time

LOW RIDER

smooth and sleek as a great blue whale
the low rider crawls down the narrow state highway

six barely visible curly heads
jolt up and down in perfect unison
to the rhythm of the shockless Chevy
tracking every wave and asphalt imperfection of the road
and I'm caught in the most frustrating position
next to introducing an old friend
whose name you've forgotten
I'm late for work and stuck
behind low riders

me pongo a reflejar
since I can't pass with the steady stream
of oncoming traffic

¿Qué es lo que sacan de esto?

is it because any speed over twenty
would send their skulls smashing through the roof?
or are they making sure the bato by the door
doesn't spill any more mota than necessary
rolling up the lid?

¿Es cosa cultural?—
are they following a blood-imprinted speed limit
set down by their abuelo's horse?
or is it just outright perversity—downright rebellion
a high-octane flexing of their machismo
(como todos tienen que seguirlos como burros)

at any rate

now that I'm slowed down I start to notice things
no había notado esa cruz en el camino
whose plastic yellow daisies
hide the stain of a spilled soul on the shoulder
y ¡qué bonita la sierra!
I've never seen the Sangre de Cristos
unfold to the cielo quite that way

and I'm in love with the irony of it all
that these batos take
the chrome-plated quadruple-headered monsters
from the Detroit technician's assembly line
and mercilessly beef up the engine even more
in order to glide down the road
idling into eternity
forcing poets behind them to forget their watches
and look at mountains

¡Orale!—ya spotearon los chamacos de Chilí
y al fin se ladean del camino para echarse unos toques

and though I'm hopelessly late
I continue putting down the road
barely in high
delicately bouncing off potholes
mirando las nubes
and building my own proud line
of blistering mad commuters

SHOWDOWN AT THE STOP AND EAT

Jesus—here he comes—
the acne-scarred needle-pocked heavy-shit dude
strutting up in a fading pattern
    como un gallo sin cola

The women have been laughing
at my poor old sombrero aguado
and he of course knows
    they're riendo at him

"Ese hippie jodido se cree la madre . . ."
    he sputters through the french fried air
"Vamos al baile en Chimayó and I'll beat the fock
out of you chingao"

And slick as a frito pie
he's back still muttering doom
in a long low blue Ford
    riddled with rusty sanding marks

the world's winner
and still mama's mean little champion

PROCOPIO

Procopio fue un muchacho muy serio
kept to himself in school
didn't chase after girls
    como los demás chamacos
pasaba todo el día
with his left foot planted up against the wall
of the Ag building
hands hitched in his pockets
hablando de su chile
    y sus becerros

Fue un soldado en Vietnam
y siempre llevaba con él un librito de rezos
que su mamá le había regalado
didn't mix much with the other guys
    wouldn't even smoke any dope
and every night after lights were long out
he'd still be mumbling softly
through the tattered pages
    soñando de su huertita

But after he lost his left leg and prayer book
to a Vietcong mine
    ya no rezaba más
and a month later when they flew him home
barely in time for his mother's velorio
    vendió todos sus becerros

Después también vendió
el terreno de su mamá
    and rented a trailer in town
which he rarely leaves
except to cash
    his monthly disability check

LITTLE EYES

DIA 24 DE JUNIO

on feast day Uncle Steven
ties a new blue handkerchief
    around his balding head
buys a pint of hundred proof
and dances the sun down
    his turtle feet gliding dreamily
several inches off the ground
turning todo el día
    like a turkey feather in the breeze

he pauses to pose for a tourist snapshot
and takes his pay
    by pulling their squinting braless daughter
out to dance
passes the entire day like that—
    sacando a todas las muchachitas más bonitas
a bailar
laughing
    while his leather-faced wife sells fry bread
a dollar each
and gets jealous

TALKING HORSES

Uncle Steven rolls his own
as we sit in the last sun
    under skeletal álamos
and talk horses

how his bitch of a mare
throws everyone except him
even if he is seventy-nine
    he's broken green horses
ribs, collarbones and legs
nearly as long as he can remember
never misses the horse races at Alcalde
where he bets half his social security
    check
on his mean-eyed appaloosa
and almost never wins

Uncle flicks the butt
into the muddy ditch
and snorts a laugh remembering
the time the movie company
hired half of San Juan
as extras in a western movie
    a couple of years back
and the director brought in a 12-gallon-hatted
Hollywood stunt man
to teach the "natives" how to ride
who first day out
got thrown on his ass right in front of the Indians
and they had to quit filming that day
    because no one could stop laughing

Uncle Steven and me
just sitting
    smoking
and talking horses

been at it for years now
but he's never once mentioned the horse
    that reared and trampled his boy

LITTLE EYES

Little Eyes
cruises down US 64
wired on weed
low and loose
as those Chimayó guys
in their springless Chevies
except he never
checks no one out
and he don't
flag no one down
at the glass-splayed
Furr's parking lot
where high school chicks
flash flabby thighs and sigh
their tight-bloused chests heaving
in pointed indifference
to the Alcalde batos
drinking Coors and Comfort
and jacking off
their hydaulics

Little Eyes
just keeps it smooth
and spaced out
straight ahead
and smokes pounds
like other people chew gum
and squirrels down
in his seat
squinting while his eyes
shrink to two brown beads
which is where
he got his nickname
because he always
walks in loaded to work
and the patients at the Rehab—
you can't fool those dudes
they've been through it
all—
well, they started asking him

why his eyes were always
so little
and the name just stuck

and Little Eyes will
probably lose his job
before long
at the Rehab
because sometimes he comes in
real
late and then he gets
the munchies
and raids the kitchen
that's supposed to be
the patients' food
but he sure is
a good counselor
well
he went through it all himself
and not so long ago
either
when he lost a year
out of his life
to the booze
just like that
and it was gone
and he don't even remember
how
except somehow he ended up
in the hospital
which was at least better
than jail
but he's a lot better
now
even though he'll drive
his old Dodge
all the way up to Picuris
just to score
a couple of joints
and he don't paint
no more

Little Eyes
is about the only one
who still goes to visit
his blind gramma
who stumbles
through the same adobe
she grew up in
and tells even better stories
than when Little Eyes
was a kid
because she gets the past
and the present
all mixed up
and talks about dead people
and plants and animals
all the same
like they was all alive
and right there
listening to her
and the family
thinks gramma's senile
and they're half scared
to go over there
so Little Eyes
is about the only one
who comes around
every day
and he likes to get stoned
before he goes
because she's even
trippier
and once he mixed
a little weed
into her Prince Albert
and she sure did talk
that day

well, it might be crazy
and a little weird sometimes
but it sure does beat
sitting in a damn bar
and anyway

Little Eyes
learns a lot
from his gramma
and he don't care
what everyone says
she's a smart old lady
funny too
and he just likes her

Gramma
likes Little Eyes too
because he comes over
and not just
on feast day
and he still talks to her
in Tewa
and mostly
she likes him
because he listens
and sometimes she'll tell grampa
what a good boy he is
just go on and on
about how he's different
from the rest
and still has
some respect
for the old ways
and though
Grampa's been dead
fourteen years
she tells him
this is the only one
that turned out
good

LOST AGAIN FOR AWHILE

she's seventeen
already tried suicide twice
(this last time with prescription drugs)
and pregnant again
though she won't even admit it to herself

the smile that once tyrannized
armies of junior high adolescents
has now frozen into a numb sneer
her eyes are always on the verge
of sinking into her face

her boy sits beside a crumbling horno
playing roughly with rocks
keeping away from everyone
and she's thinking about getting lost again
for awhile
Albuquerque—Gallup maybe
but she'll be back
the child-support check blown
cursing her mother
through the locked screen door

she's Uncle Steven's granddaughter
who he showed how to twist the reeds
and mix the clay
the girl with the crow-black eyes
he taught to tie her moccasins
and dance the butterfly
the one he told all the old stories to
so they wouldn't be forgotten

A DOLLAR NINETY-EIGHT

They call her "a dollar ninety-eight"
after the TV show of the same name
that featured middle-aged housewives
parading down an aisle in straining bikinis
competing for a grand prize of a buck ninety-eight
and national overexposure on the tube
and maybe because she thinks she stands out
like a queen with her curly blond hair
and nearly blue eyes
among the earthen faces of the pueblo
and maybe because Leonard's aunts think his "prize"
is worth about that much (even considering inflation)
they all call her "a dollar ninety-eight"
and Leonard's been going with her for a year now.

Last summer he cut off all five toes on his left foot
working with a chain saw for the Youth Conservation Corps
up on Santa Clara Peak
but he's learned how to hobble along on his toeless stump
and he gets around pretty good
for a guy with half a foot and a white girlfriend.

ANSWER

"You get yourself an axe
an hachazuela and a hatchet
find yourself a fallen cottonwood
cut off a big chunk of the trunk
hitch up the horse and haul it back
hollow the damn thing out by hand
little by little—it'll probably take you
a couple of weeks
then file down the rough spots
sand it a little
maybe even carve a sun or an eagle
in the front there
if you've got a hand for it
then set it someplace
no one's likely to move it
for a couple hundred years
get a bucket
fill it from the ditch
and water the cattle and goats in it"

        answered Uncle Steven
        when I asked him how a man
        could possibly hope to be remembered
        after he's gone

LOS CUMPLEAÑOS DE DOÑA AGUEDA

SUEÑO

si tú me besas
con tus ojos
¿cómo no querré tus labios también?
cuando me llamaste
en una risa clara
y peligrosamente íntima
pues tuve que ser dueño
de tu boca—¡ay!—de tu mero resuello
pero me arrimé muy cerca
queriendo pescarte
con mis manos torpes de realidad
y con una vuelta desapareciste
dejándome solo entre flores de nopal
sin ningún remedio más
que las piedras blancas y pervertidas
de mi pobre poesía

11 DE JULIO

el día 11 de julio
palomas are skimming
off the jeweled rocío de la madrugada
today man-made shrapnel
will rain down del cielo

el caballo entero
está rodando en el suelo
clouds of dust billow gold
in the breaking sun
our best friends
are talking about the impending holocaust
when there will be no more food or fuel
y el dinero no valdrá nada
they are preparing
by opening a savings account
esta mañana las nubes son japonesas

down the road don Agustín
está cumpliendo noventa y seis años
he walks with a cane
y habla sin medida de su Señor Jesucristo
who keeps him around to demonstrate
how insignificant centuries are

LOS CUMPLEAÑOS DE DOÑA AGUEDA

ya doña Agueda ha llegado a un lugar
donde la edad no se figura por años
sino por agua y tierra

las arrugas que el Río del Oso
corta en los médanos
cuando corre una vez cada generación
son iguales a las de su cara

ha sembrado chile siempre
y las calles que doña Agueda ha escardado
son más largas que todos los caminos
que andarás en tu vida

las jergas que hace de garras torcidas
tejen siglos
trenzando chiste con calavera
madrugada con medianoche

ahora su hija le está buscando un novio
para celebrar el día de su santo
    "pero le dije que me buscara un joven
    porque los pelados ya no traen nada"
pero la dificultad—como todos saben—
no consiste en conseguir compañeros
sino en sacarla de su huerta suficiente tiempo
para tener un "party"

son los cumpleaños de doña Agueda
y cuando ya no ande por sus matitas de chile
los álamos en la acequia se callarán

se secará otra raíz
de nuestra pasado destejido

ROOSTER GARCIA

no one can beat the Tewas for nicknames
everyone in the pueblo
(and even the regular outsider)
gets tagged with an additional name
that sticks with him from conception
to the funeral reception
replacing the proper baptismal appellation
on grade school report cards
and local police blotters
even etching eventually into gravestone granite
like skinny knobby-kneed "Grasshopper Legs"
or the dark-skinned "Coffee"
or the blond fair-faced Vista volunteer
who came to elevate the pueblo's awareness with tips
on nutrition and child care
she had picked up on a Peace Corps stint in Zambia
and who was rapidly dubbed "The African"
or "Crouch" the local Casanova
who was preoccupied with tight-fitting levi's
and the female nether anatomy
and who but for a benevolent mispronunciation
would have gone through life as "Crotch"

but fate didn't even allow "Rooster" García
the common courtesy of a nickname
somewhat related to his physical characteristics
or personal foibles
for the name Rooster was cast
even before the fetus jiggled in the womb
as it was fairly common knowledge
his mother was having an affair with "Hermano Herminio"
the big blustering Alleluia preacher
who one day arrived
in "God's great and powerful whirlwind"
as he liked to say
though what really happened
is that his dented and disintegrating 47 Chevy
exhausted from the eternal search for souls
and the "Almighty's handiwork on earth"
finally rattled and wheezed and went

to its eternal reward
right outside Chamita

and even though they changed
the locations of their feverish rendezvous
frequently enough to keep Hermano Herminio
in a state of constant confusion
as to whether he was going to a certain place
to pray for the "Good Lord's bountiful blessings"
or to receive them
the kids, in an unceasing effort to augment
their ongoing education
followed Hermano Herminio and his illicit Eve around
once having the good fortune
of witnessing the entire thing through the cracks
between the slats of Uncle Steven's chicken house
out in back of the convent and those who were missing
from the gang were called over to watch
the whole ageless ritual
from the impatient fumbling with stubborn clothes
to the joyful moans
and Hermano Herminio's strange prayer afterwards
a curious mix of penitence and thanksgiving
he offered to the Holy Shepherd
while kneeling still naked in the hay

Rooster of course was the resultant fruit
of the chicken coop seeding
and never having a prayer of a chance
to live it down
rather early in his life
decided to live up to his name
becoming one of the meanest and struttingest gallos
in all of San Juan
breaking many a heart
busting numerous heads
and fathering a long line of anonymous children
until finally in his forties he changed his ways
married a widow from Santa Clara
and settled down on his mother's ranch
to raise hay and racing horses
and Rooster was happy and pretty successful later on
leaving all of his past behind
except of course his name

FRIGID

"Oye—¿qué es frigid?"
    pregunta mamá

ha aguantado todo el programa
bien calladita
pero ya tiene que saber por qué
todos están manejando esa palabra
con tanto cuidado y temor

unos tres años pasados
no habría pensado uno
que mamá dejaría los trastes y la escoba
para sentarse una hora a cuidar los "monos"
en la televisión

pero mira—ya está como un tecato
con su "soap opera"
y yo y papá ni entramos a lonchar
hasta que se acabe otro día
de problemas y tristeza
de la pobre gente de mamá

bueno—está bien que descanse un poco
al cabo que está aprendiendo mucho
de su historia
ya habla de las "lesbians" y "battered wives"
hasta sabe algo de "schizophrenia"
nomás que cada rato me espanta
cuando me dice:
    "¿Supites que se murió el Larry hoy?"
y yo pensando en mi cuñado—
otra vez me estaba platicando
de como el David y la Linda habían hecho "golpe"
(su expresión para la movida)
y yo estaba cierto que al fin
habían pescado a mi primo "chiteando"

no—claro que todos son de la familia
de los "days of our lives"
y he aceptado que esos días
ya son también de nuestra vida

pero lo que quiero saber yo
es cómo le va a traducir "frigid" a papá
(él dice que no tiene ningún interés en "esas
    pendejadas"—pero cada día pregunta por sus
    favoritos)

¿le va a decir que la Susan "se heló"—
o que ya no "golpea" como antes?

EL HAMBRE EN LA LUNA

Hace años que los Estados Unidos
gastó suficiente dinero
para darle de comer a la mitad del mundo
muriéndose de hambre
que nunca vemos
y puso un hombre
en la luna

Ahora los mismos pobres
y sus niños
siguen muriéndose
por falta de pan
y los científicos justifican
su gran gasto de dinero
con los beneficios
que han resultado
del programa Apollo
como el descubrimiento
de materiales nuevos
conque están haciendo
mejores ollas hoy en día
para preparar la comida
que papá dice
que nos va a faltar
también a nosotros
un día de éstos
porque está predicho
en la Biblia
pero nosotros
los suertudos
comeremos por un tiempo
de los elotes
y frijoles del jardín
hasta que los malvados vienen
a quitarnos la cosecha
con sus carabinas—
papá también jura
que no anduvo
un hombre en la luna
que todo ese barullo

fue una mentira
puros retratos
en la televisión—
es imposible
que un hombre
anduviera en la luna
porque sólo Dios
puede andar por las estrellas
y eso
como el hambre
nunca cambiará

MAS LEJOS QUE GERMANY

estaba allí atrás en la despensa
leyendo cartas
que su papá le había mandado
cuando estaba en germany
en la primera guerra—
hay un retrato de él
con su uniforme y chinos
en el cuarto poblado con retratos
en todas las paredes
y arriba de los muebles
que se quedaron en el mismo lugar
donde siempre estaban
cuando tenía su esposa viva todavía—
aquí se crió toda la familia
en esta vieja casa tan grande
y tan vacía ahora
que tiene que salirse a buscar las cartas
que su papá le mandó
cuando fue soldado
leyendo en la despensa
más lejos ya que germany

DE COLORES

De colores
son los pajarillos
que vienen de afuera

"¡Ay Diosito—aquel de allá
porque el de aquí es americano!"
    dice tía Lucía
cuando ya no aguanta las pendejadas
de los mormones

"¿Quién te hace quedarte en Utah?"
    le pregunta papá
su único hermano

"Pues, tienes razón, nito"
    responde ella—
y hasta ganas tengo de volver a mi tierra
donde no me tratarían como una extranjera
pero aquí tengo mi casa—aquí trabajó mi esposo
toda su vida, y aquí me voy a morir también

Pero aquí ni la raza habla español
el Safeway no vende posole
y no hay misa en español
Pero siempre tía Lucía al madrugarse
agarra su rosario y le reza en mexicano a su Diosito
aquel de allá
porque este americano blanco de aquí
piensa que manda todo el mundo
pero ella sabe que su Dios verdadero
pinta el cielo de colores
y canta por los pájaros en mil lenguajes

TU ERES EL MAR

Quisiera saborear tu boca
y perder mis dedos por la vida
en tu cabello negro
   ¿Cómo que me pescaste
   con una sóla mirada?
   ¡Qué ojos tan fuertes
   que me hechizaron con su linda y rara
   brujería!
Quisiera abandonarme en tus brazos
como el sol cayéndose en el mar
   Moriré alegremente para despertarme
   en las ondas secretas de tu cuerpo

UNA MUJER ELECTRICA

doña Eulalia es "una mujer muy eléctrica"
como dice mamá—
la pobre viejita ya ha enterrado a tres esposos
pero está buscando su cuarto
nomás que a sus ochenta y tres años
siempre es física
y no va a brincar al primer viudo
que todavía tiene sus clavijas

"el otro día me vino un hombre a solicitarme"
    nos dice
"pero no me cuadró—tenía un lunar muy feo
aquí en el cachete"

mientras que sus amigas se hallan en casas de ancianos
doña Eulalia se levanta a las seis de la mañana
para bañarse
echándose perfume de su colección de "taboo" y "my sin"
peinándose con unas peinetas bonitas
ya lista para las ocho
pa' escuchar "quién se murió" en el radio
y a prenderse con su hija o nieta
para ir a la plaza donde pasará por T.G.&Y.
con su ojo de águila bien pelado
en busca de un soltero elegible
y hay buenas esperanzas que lo halle
como nunca ha quedado viuda más de nueve meses—
pues cuando se murió su segundo marido
ella se fue hasta México buscando otro querido
(quizás la cosecha de hombres locales
ya estaba bien pepenada)
y sí pronto vino pa'trás con un hombre trigueño
cerca de la mitad de su edad
pero ése falleció después de cáncer
y doña Eulalia se quedó
"otra vez"—como dice ella—'en la movida"

"es una mujer muy eléctrica"
dicen las vecinas con una risa
y también un poco de envidia

FRANKIE

like the war in which he fought
Frankie's all but forgotten now
buried in the State Pinta
near ancient Cerrillos turquoise mines
he passes the day building his biceps
and writing his mama who still subsists
on the old family ranch
he was an Eagle Scout
made president of the student council
and escorted the dark-eyed prom queen
always friendly
Frankie was everybody's favorite
but after the war something—
it was barely noticeable at first—
had changed
he could still be prodded into laughter
at the Saints and Sinners Bar
but the edge of a snarl had crept into his laugh
he still shot the best game of eight ball
this side of the río
but now he could no longer tolerate losing
and Frankie who had slapped more backs
in his tender years than the majority of the políticos
of Río Arriba County
grew morose when he drank
withdrawn and dangerously quiet
and incredulous vecinos kept the casual acquaintances
and twice-removed relatives on the phone all day
wondering if it was the same Frankie Sandoval
the *Santa Fe New Mexican*
reported as being one of two men who
after an altercation outside the Senate Lounge
had followed a Louisiana man to his motel room
where they bludgeoned him to death with a tire iron
and some folks rather cynically remarked
that it just proved Frankie really did have
all his marbles—
in fact was still a pretty wily character—
when he'd suddenly fling his hands over his face
in the courtroom to escape the terrible caras

of the evil spirits hurling into his eyes
and maybe they were right
because after a six-month stint
at the State Mental Hospital
Frankie one morning woke up sane enough
to be resentenced to the Pen
(if you can call that "sane")
but I still believe it was the war—
the napalm—the smack—
the blood-gutted flies that did it—
the war that no one remembers
like the honor student in Block 3, Cell 52

LOS ABUELOS

escóndete hijito
los abuelos vienen
con sus máscaras
y sus manos gigantes
te van a pescar
te van a llevar
al pozo sin fondo de la medianoche—
tú sabes que no te has portado bien
anoche le hablaste mal a tu mamá
ayer pegaste a tu hermanita—
rezar debajo de las cobijas
no te va a valer
vienen los abuelos a buscarte
con sus azotes y dientes afilados
y no puedes huir hijito
tú nunca escaparás

ENTRO ABUELITO PASANDO COMO UNA SOMBRA

entró abuelito pasando como una sombra
y estos carajos ni nos presentaron

manos que hicieron estos adobes
espalda que se dobló
a levantar estas paredes
alma que colgó estas vigas arriba de nuestras cabezas
pasando ahora por su propia casa como una sombra
y su nieto y los amigos de él—
estos profesores, poetas y artistas
pasando el vino y los bultos y los libros
que han creado del espíritu de este mismo anciano
que ignoraron como un peón
en el castillo de los poderosos
sin ofrecerle la mano
sin darle tan siquiera las buenas noches de Dios

siguieron tomando estos santeros
contando sus chistes y platicando de su santo arte
mientras que abuelito pasó como una sombra
andando con pasos lentos y tiesos
a su cuarto en la orilla de la casa
donde se quedó el resto de la noche
solito, sentado en su cama
encerrado adentro de un anillo invisible de pájaros
    callados

HAROLD M. ES RATA

LOS HERMANOS RETARDED

Todos los días los veo
trudging to mass
the sister
    less severely retarded
always a few hundred feet
ahead of her brother
who struggles along
    in a waterless breaststroke
wavering off his shorter right leg
utterly oblivious
to the commuters squealing past
    up the hill
or the packs of schoolchildren
who stare in rare silence
even the Corucotown dogs
grant them exclusive passage rights
without venturing a bark
for they've been here forever
    "los hermanos retarded"
sure as the sun
crawling like vines toward the light
climbing inexorably past heaven and hell
to their mysterious blank-eyed reunion
    with the Lord

LOS DESAPARECIDOS Y NO PUEDEN DESAPARECERSE MAS

Los desaparecidos ya no pueden desaparecerse más
porque los que nunca vuelven jamás podrán despedirse
y la pena de los perdidos se multiplicará en los rostros
de las madres que marchan en la plaza inundada
    por su mismo dolor

Chuang Tsu soñó ser mariposa y cuando despertó
no podía figurar si él era el hombre
que había soñado ser mariposa
o si era la mariposa que ahora soñaba ser hombre

Pero los generales nunca duermen
ni mucho menos permiten soñar
y la Argentina ha llegado a ser la pesadilla
de sus hijos desaparecidos
lo mismo como los Estados Unidos es la amarga visión
de los indios enterrados bajo sus llanos
    de trigo y olvido

ABUELA

abuela is the last drop of candlelight
in the empty iglesia
after the priest's drained his bottle
    and collapsed into bed

she's manzanilla and mastranzo
tortillas at dawn
and endlessly spinning woolen rezos
that save us all

                                she's hard homemade jabón
lyeing out every iniquity

es la primera para llegar a misa
front pew middle aisle
next to doña Emilia
                        and she tape records
the homily
on her Sears cassette
tucked neatly into her bolsa
to play back hours later
        over foggy Sunday morning blanquillos y chile

as a remedio
for our inevitable Saturday night sins

HANDS

in the year my eyes were level
with the doorknob
my father would walk so far away
that when he came back he'd be a giant
    with his hands of so large and silent a love
    with his hands so scarred by water and earth
cracked like he washed them in lightning

and now a hand that has held nothing but pencil
holds this page
    so smooth and unmarked a hand
that has never held love but as a book
                        at a readable
distance

and my father's mother
who lost all the songs of her mother
in the shell of that ship in the atlantic
and her husband on his knees
in the beet fields of colorado
    dreaming in alien tongues of the rhine
bentbacked and mute in their bedroom at night
barely sustaining their bodies through time
see
    those hands
that held nothing (between them) a colorless flower
bursts from the fingers

HAROLD M. ES RATA

"Harold M. es rata"
   reads the huge spray-painted message
marqueed on the east wall of T.G.&Y.
in the Big Rock Shopping Center
where lowriders slither together
panzas rascando
                  while barechested hermaphrodites
shake glamorous locks
blink tragic lids and curse the universe
outside their furry cockpits
                  and every abuelita
from Tierra Azul down to Corucotown understands
that "Harold M. es rata"
   (pobrecito)
sacudiendo la cabeza
as they elbow through the clutch of comadres
to grab their best buy on toilet paper and buy a get-well
card for the vecina's husband
                  who lies wheezing
terminal breath
in C-Ward at the Presbyterian Hospital
his stomach heaving and abruptly collapsing
   and cheerleaders giggle
in the shaded portal
hounding Safeway carryouts to buy
a dozen home-baked brownies so they can finance
   their next trip to the cheering clinic in Roswell
                  and they flash
brace-glinted sonrisas
and wonder what the "M" stands for
   and does anybody even *know* a Harold anyway?
pero Harold M. no es rata
es gordo nomás
big as a carnival and rigorously silent
Harold M. is only fat
                  which
you will remember
is just about the worst thing you can be

in high school

EAT GOOD

"Eat good"
     she said
seating us in our shift around the long kitchen table
but this year Wayne-Boy didn't dance the deer
this year Wayne-Boy was shot through the heart
in front of a bar

"Eat good"
     she said
spooning more garbanzos and thin red chile
into the ollas on the table
for it was feast day
the family was home
and Father Roca said we must accept our crosses of
suffering
in Christ-like resignation

"Eat good"
     she said
slicing pastelitos for the anxious grandchildren
and handing around thick bizcochitos
smiling while her bones still wailed for Wayne-Boy

HIDDEN BEHIND THE STACKS

I was hidden behind the stacks
at the Holy Cross High School Library
reading a declassified copy
of the Los Alamos Scientific Laboratory's
Manhattan Project report
when the following conversation between two
student aides
filtered through the almanacs
and Compton's Picture Encyclopedias

"Anda—dame un besito."
   "No, I can't."
"Anda—nomás un besito chiquito."
   "No, no puedo. What'll Vicente say?"
"Aw, how's he gonna know?"
   "No, I gotta go now. Mrs. Martínez—she don't trust
me."
"Anda, mujer—just a little besito."

At which point she finally gave in
though apparently without much conviction

"Ooh—¡qué besito tan seco! ¡Dame otro!"

But one was all he would get—for now at least
and the coy muchachita came scampering around
the corner and disappeared down the nonfiction aisle
while I returned to my report
and read that on the morning of August 9, 1945
Major C.W. Sweeney
pilot of the strike ship "Great Artiste"
was forced to scrub the primary target of Kokura
because the Japanese city was "obscured
by heavy ground haze and smoke"
and proceeded instead to Nagasaki
where Bomb Commander Ashworth dropped
the "Fat Man" on an anonymous adolescent
stealing kisses hidden behind the stacks
at the high school library

PATRIA

Nuevo México
   tierra anciana de mesas acabadas
   como la quijada del viejo molacho
tierra también de montañas ricas e inexploradas
como los pechos de una joven

Nuevo México
   patria de los hispanos
   que siguen hablando el idioma de su herencia
por el barullo incesante del inglés
   pueblo de los indios
que todavía bailan el Búfalo y el Venado
rodeados de turistas tejanos

Hogar eres también
   mi Nuevo México
de la bomba atómica
destructor de mundos

Cuna de la primera gente
   el Anasazi de las leyendas más antiguas
tú también posees la llave terrible
del apocalipsis

Tú eres el único tren rumbo a la madrugada
pero sólo vendes boletos expirados
   Nuevo México
eres un puente perdido entre los pinos

VET

Fidel wants to talk about it
    but he can't
so he pounds bear claws
into 20-gauge silver
with a rawhide mallet
and solders fine bezels
around the turquoise silence
that never stops whispering
in his mother's voice
begging him to come home
                please
come back home alive

And then he said
    You wanna play for ten bucks
And I said
    Sure, but why don't we play for twenty
And he said
    Okay
But I said
    Let's see your twenty first before we start
And I called Old Mike over
and made him hold the money
But then that Spanish guy said
    Okay then, why don't we shoot for fifty
Well, I knew I was better than him
so I said
    Okay, but you gotta give your money to Old Mike
    here to hold
And he said
    What's the matter, don't you trust me
And I said
    No
Well, I don't trust you either
    He said
And I don't trust that old Indian there
Well, that's when I got mad
And I said
    Do you wanna go outside maybe
And he said
    No, but how about we play for a hundred bucks
And I said
    How about we go outside and I'll just beat
    the hundred bucks outa you
And he said
    You see all them guys sitting there
    They're all my friends and they don't like Indians
    too much either
So that's when I broke my cuestick over his head
But them Spanish guys sure do fight dirty
One guy tried to hold me down while that other one
who wanted to shoot for a hundred bucks kicked me
but I got him back too

and I bet you his nose is pretty crooked now
But the bad thing was
Old Mike took off with my twenty
    dammit
And he's supposed to be my friend

POETICA REVOLUCIONARIA

El poema empieza a gritar
cuando los tiros acaban
    con el silencio

Solloza como un niño desconsolado
cuando los niños olvidan las lágrimas
por tanto llorar

Tartamudea en sílabas mochas
cuando la metáfora se ahoga
    en la sangre del pobre

El poema al fin deja ser
    poema

Escondido en el hueco del corazón
se convierte en un cuchillo de plata
    que sólo corta y corta

y corta

JESUS IN THE TORTILLA

I wouldn't laugh at Jesus in the tortilla
if I were you

That lineman thought he'd prove the Cristo that appeared
mysteriously in the rocks above Ojo Caliente was a hoax
so he blackmarketed some explosives
and blew the vision to granite dust right under the noses
of all those superstitious women
and it's said that less than a week later
he somehow grabbed hold of a hot line and hung there
for a horrible sizzling instant
before they could cut the juice and pull him loose
and though he did make it through intensive care
at Saint Jo's
he ended up losing both arms above the elbows

And then there was that bato in Mora
who grew tired of the constant circus
camped in front of the wall where Christ appeared
in the ripples of the plaster
attended by the Virgin, a lamb, or the devil himself
lurking in the jaspe shadows—all depending
on the prejudice of the viewer's eye—
so he hit on the idea of blackening the idol's face
with a little fire he'd fashion out of kerosene and rags
but as he came driving down the canyon
he lost control of his truck
smashing into a concrete embankment
and barely escaping with his life
when the kerosene on the seat beside him ignited
leaving him with severe burns over his upper torso
and face

So even though they're selling tacos, postcards
and authentic blessed tortillas
and the archbishop himself has pilgrimaged down
to gawk at the holy dough
I wouldn't laugh so hard at Jesus in the tortilla
and for awhile
I'd be careful of what I ate

EL VECINO

Dawn and don Belarmino
    el vecino de noventa y tres años
has already finished his morning cafecito
and inched out the door to his woodpile
where he splits the sawmill tailings
that seem to levitate to his motionless hacha

"Buenos días le dé Dios"
    he salutes all the neighbors
and the words crystallize and hang in the crisp air
like cotton plumes from the álamos
that line the acequia don Belarmino himself
must have dug
palada by patient palada back in the days
when God was still laying out the rivers

PETRA JR.

Petra Jr. scavenges the streets
like her namesake and predecessor
funnel-eyed and spindly as Sebastiana
she glides along
a starched hallucination
on the gravelly fringes of Corucotown
paralyzing dogs and bewitching ripe fetuses

defamatory talk actually
as she's probably no more than an ordinary orphan
yet you can't deny
she outruns most makes of automobiles
like Petra herself did in her prime
riding the prevailing winds into the village ahead of you
and she loosens the stones out of children's hands
with the same withering glance
the old resident hechicera once used to wilt roses
and inspire frantic signs of the cross

but we need her
delineating the edge with fear on the shoulders
we must have her
porque sin la bruja no hay santos

it's dark roots that keep the tree alive

EN EL PRIMER ANIVERSARIO DEL ASESINATO DEL ARZOBISPO ROMERO

Hace un año
que mataron al arzobispo Arnulfo Romero
en el mero altar
          Dios te salve United Brands
          la CIA es contigo
          bendita eres entre todas las compañías
          y manchado es el dinero de tu bolsa
          con sangre
Hoy en este día
Washington prometió sesenta y tres millones
de dólares más
al gobierno de El Salvador
          Santa Proctor & Gamble
          madre de miseria
          crece por nosotros
          los asesinos
          a pesar y a provecho
          de la gente indígena
Y mientras que la prensa unida
sigue sumando las muertes
el presidente Reagan se ahinca en la iglesia a rezar
en contra
del terrorismo internacional
          en el nombre Del Monte
          y del ESSO y del espíritu
          de Coca-Cola
No lloren madrecitas
     los muertos están bien protegidos
No se apene querido papá
     nunca se harán comunistas

ROOTS

Coyote parked his van
in the middle of the pueblo
and set off scouring mesas
for a living
searching for some sign of the first ones
a bottlecap
a fossilized watch perhaps
but he always stole back at night
to calibrate the kiva
and water the prickly pears
growing on his roof
until one morning
Uncle Steven's great-granddaughter
caught Coyote sniffing for his wallet
and asked him:
   "Are you from somewhere?"
and Coyote knew
it was one of those questions
that would just stick with him
forever

EL PADRE VERDADERO

> *Dame un misa cantada*
> *y rezada con el humo*
> *saliendo del guajo y con*
> *todas las pendejaditas*

Father Christensen was a man God built
to be a priest
        un padre verdadero

With eyebrows knit like Moses and arms thick
as a horse's neck
Father Christensen towered over the tallest teenager
in the San José procession
    his great cassock flapping
                      a black eagle
in the March wind

He loved pageantry and all the pendejaditas
and though his marathon masses calcified generations
    of kneecaps
everyone loved him
porque hablaba mexicano and he liked his green chile
y hasta sus buenos tragos se echaba
    de vez en cuando

But it was more than his stature
and his barrelly risa and the ballpark he built
where he himself a veces agarraba la pelota para jugar
    al béisbol con los chamaquitos
Father Christensen was loved because he looked
    and acted
just like abuela said a real padre should

Naturally he also invaded your privacy like a real father
    as well
entering every house in the parish without knocking
and generously inviting himself to dinner, announcing:
    "Mejor llegar a tiempo que ser convidado"
and once he even caught doña Petrita's hija
coming out of the shower forcing her to drip dry
    in the closet

Pero a pesar de sus faltas
Father Christensen was infinitely better
than this crewcut chaparrito que tenemos ahora
que ni a los old regulars en el primer banco conoce
and who plows through the missal like it was
        a telephone book
demystifying cada misterio
and even dispensing with the sign of peace

SUFFOCATING

"Have I been married forever?"
    Gloria sighs to herself
removing the diaper as delicately
as José once unhooked her bra
    he had been so gentle with her so
protective
and she swallows hard and remembers horseback rides
through the arroyos west of Corucotown
pursued by laughing neighborhood
boys and wide-mouthed kisses in sandstone caves
    and the rose
on that first anniversary that never opened
only the bottom petal peeled away but the bud
    had remained frozen in a crimson knot and Gloria
brushes her long fine hair while the washing machine
gurgles and the baby cries herself to sleep
    hair
that once danced in the wind as she galloped her red mare
over the jagged mesas and she ties it back to knead
the masa for tomorrow's tortillas and tries to remember
    how to breathe

MAYORDOMO

the mayordomo parks his 58 Dodge pickup
with the battered barandal and the caved-in door
in the center of the camino
    jellies through the barbed wire fence
snagging a rip in the back of his ancient leva
and walks up with his eternal mud-packed shovel
    slung over his shoulder
trailed by his arthritic German Shepherd
and I know I'm in for a two-hour recitation
of the unabridged oral history of the Salazar Ditch
complete with the flood of 29 and the drought of 48
along with a half-dozen chistes about his latest
    rendezvous with the viuda María
and the inevitable condemnation of the lazy sonofabitch
muchachos de hoy en día who won't even touch a pala
    for fifteen bucks a day anymore

the mayordomo gestures and gesticulates the hours away
with his dedo mocho
    the stub of a right index finger
sacrificed decades ago to a band saw
while his shaggy cejas dance over his watery eyes
and he reaches for the petrified wad of Juicy Fruit gum
stuck over the bill of his grease-stained cachucha
    and though the sun has sizzled into shadows
and I've spent the entire afternoon simply nodding my
    head
I finally pay my acequia fee
content the ritual has been accomplished

warm winds can stir in the cottonwoods again
history remains intact
the compuertas will soon be flooding open

NUNCA TE VOY A DECIR

Nunca te voy a decir mi nombre de verdad
porque pudieras robarlo
echarlo en tu caja de plomo
arrastrarlo por el suelo
en la luz de la luna helada
y picarlo con agujas largas
de acero relumbroso

Por eso
nunca te voy a decir mi nombre
aunque piensas que ya lo sabes

LA SIRENA DEL RIO GRANDE

Había una sirena en el Río Grande
    decía mamá
the spirit of the river
she haunted the Russian olive shore
singing to the moon
and bewitching innocent boys
    unimaginably beautiful
nomás la mirabas
y te volvías esclavo de ella
    abandoning your wife
to listen to her silvery song
forgetting your children
    for a chance to explore
the liquid curves of her body

Pero eso fue en los tiempos de antes
before Ronald Warner brought his cranes and shovels
to dredge her delicate lips
    before steel and concrete beams
burst her secret virginity
    before they constructed the sewage treatment plant

Ahora huyó la Sirena del Río Grande
y ya anda por ahí en México
but she left her sister behind
    La Llorona
who wails at the freshly frozen moon
and traps living creatures
    with her bottomless eyes
La Malinche se llama
and she is our spirit of the river
    and her song is sure madness
and her body swollen death

GRANDFATHER KNOWS

grandfather knows
    that the world's about to end
because the Bible says so
    at least his copy does
and he knows
    the moon landing was filmed in Arizona
and he can tell you
    all the cycles of the moon
and how you have to plant roots
    when the horns are down
and chile when the crescent's up
    but never castrate a calf
when the moon is full
    for it might bleed to death
and grandfather knows
    how to weave a rope
out of horse hair
    and the best knot to tie the horse up
and there's nothing he can't tell you
    about irrigation or communism
or overhauling a tractor with baling wire
    in fact no one knows
more than grandfather
    why he even
fixed up this poem for me
    erasing all the best lines

Glossary

The following is a partial list of dialectical Spanish terms used in the poems. For further information, consult: *A Dictionary of New Mexico and Southern Colorado Spanish*, Rubén Cobos, Museum of New Mexico Press, Santa Fe, 1983.

ARREAR: To drive a car or vehicle.

ASINA: Colonial New Mexico Spanish spelling of *así*, "in that manner," "thus."

CHITEANDO: Slang term, "cheating."

CHOTA: Slang term, "cop."

ECHARSE UNOS TOQUES: To "toke up," i.e., to smoke marijuana.

ENPAPÁ: A term of endearment and respect for one's father. Origin unclear, though santero and Spanish instructor Félix López speculates the term may be a shortened form of an earlier expression, *en papá confío*—"in my father I trust."

ESCURO: Colonial New Mexico Spanish spelling of *oscuro*, "dark."

ESTAMPAS: Food stamps.

FÍSICA: Picky, particular.

HACHAZUELA: Spanish diminutive of *hacha*, "hatchet," "small axe."

JALE: Slang term for job, work.

JEFE: Slang term for the "old man," i.e., father.

LEMITAS: A tart, lemonlike wild berry in northern New Mexico.

LONCHAR: Slang term, "to eat lunch."

MONO: Slang term for movies, show.

MOVIDA: On the move, on the make (sexual connotation).

NADIEN: Colonial New Mexico Spanish spelling of *nadie*, "nobody."

NITO: Spanish diminutive of *hermanito*, "brother." Almost always used in a negative, ironic manner, as in "No, nito."

PEPENADA: Picked over.

PRENDERSE: To tag along.

QUINCE: In the expression, *ir pa'l quince*, to be "all wrong," "all messed up."

RASTRILLO: Hay rake.

TORTILLAS MEXICANAS: Tortillas prepared with whole-wheat flour.